So You're Adopted

So You're Adopted

Fred Powledge

Charles Scribner's Sons
New York

Copyright © 1982 Fred Powledge

Library of Congress Cataloging in Publication Data

Powledge, Fred.
So you're adopted.
Bibliography: p.
Includes index.
Summary: Examines the personal concerns and
questions that sometimes trouble adopted
youngsters and their families. Also discusses
the social and legal aspects of adoption.
1. Adoption—Juvenile literature. 2. Children,
Adopted—Juvenile literature. 3. Adoptees—Juvenile literature.
4. Adoptees
—Identification—Juvenile literature.
[1. Adoption] I. Title. II. Title: So you
are adopted.
HV875.P69   362.7'34   81-23278
ISBN 0-684-17347-6   AACR2

3 5 7 9 11 13 15 17 19 F/C 20 18 16 14 12 10 8 6 4 2

Printed in the United States of America

For
Pauline and Arlius Powledge,
my parents

Contents

So You're Adopted

One

Something Special

So you're adopted. Does that make you somehow *special?*

Apparently it does, even though, when you think about how many other adoptees there are in the world, being adopted doesn't seem so terribly unusual at all. There are millions of people on Earth who were adopted, and millions more are in the process of being adopted, and millions more will someday be adopted. All of these people, like you, have been (or will be) born, and then for one reason or another will be separated from their biological parents, and then will become the legal members of other families, with all the same rights and privileges and obligations of children who were actually born into those families.

This system of adoption, or some variation on it, has been going on for as long as we've had civilized societies on our planet, and it's very likely to continue far into the future. The system involves a very large number of people.

1

So why is it that people who've been adopted can consider themselves *special* when there are so many other people in the same situation? And how is it that someone can feel special about an event in his or her life that may have occurred even before it could be remembered—often in the very first days? How is it that many people who were adopted (possibly *most* people who were adopted) seem to have a special corner in their hearts—in that undefinable place that's part memory, part feelings, part intelligence—that is reserved for the knowledge that *I'm adopted?*

The writer of this book was adopted more than forty-five years ago. A lot of things have happened to me in that time (fortunately, the great majority of them have been good things), and very few of them have had anything directly to do with adoption. I learned the games of childhood, found that I needed eyeglasses, skinned my knees and elbows, had a dog named Blackie, went to school, served in the Army, got married, started a career, got a ticket for speeding, learned to love spinach, became a father, broke my arm, bought a canoe, learned how to cook Chinese food, and did a lot of other things that were equally important or unimportant. And yet there is a small place tucked away in me that is permanently reserved for thoughts about being adopted: a place that says, *Yes, there* is *something special about being adopted.*

And it says this even though there is another part of me that keeps reminding me that being adopted is just one of the many components that have been mixed together over the years to make me what I am. We know very little about the feelings and thoughts that adopted people have, but everything we do know seems to point to the notion that adopted people do have some special feelings that nonadopted people don't have. This is not to say that there's something wrong with those feelings; it's just that they are special.

Two

Protection

People have been adopting children for a very long time—certainly as far back as our recorded history goes, and probably a lot farther than that, into the times when there were people on Earth but no way to write down and preserve the records of their dealings with each other.

Adoption back then was pretty much the same thing that it is now, although there may not have been quite so many legal documents to sign and forms to fill out. Basically, what adoption meant, and still means, is that someone (the adoptive couple) is promising to assume all the responsibilities for taking care of someone else—feeding him, providing his clothes and shelter, assisting him through the years of childhood and preparing him for adult life, providing for his education, trying to explain the differences between right and wrong, good and evil, night and day, apples and oranges, dogs and cats, and all the millions of other things that go into what we call "bringing somebody up"

4

or "rearing" him. In other words, the people who do the adopting (in most but not all cases they are married couples) are promising to enroll the adopted person in their family.

It is a full-fledged, no-strings-attached membership, with no special rules just for adopted members, and no special privileges either. The adopted person becomes a member of the family, legally and in every other way. There are no provisions for returning an adoptee after a one-year trial period or whatever, any more than other children come with guarantees. This family membership is almost always issued voluntarily, because the adopting people *want* to make a place in their lives for the adoptee. The meaning of the word "adopt" is "to choose," and that's exactly what it means.

Once the adoption takes place, and is recognized legally (usually by a simple, written order from a judge), the adopted person *is* a member of the adoptive family, with all the rights and obligations of any other young person in that family. She or he takes not only the family name, but also the family's very *identity*—so that when someone talks about going to visit "the Williamses" or "the Garcias," they mean *all* the Williamses or the Garcias, not just those who were born directly into that family. If someone remarks that "The Steins ought to do something about their dog; he barked all night last night," the criticism gets shared by all the Steins, whether they are adopted or not. Of course, this identity business works both ways; the family into which an adopted child comes will be shaped and influenced, in part, by the characteristics and contributions that that child makes, too.

From the very beginning of the recorded history of adoption, the idea behind the practice was to protect children who, for one reason or another, were without protection. The reason might be that the child's parents had died, or that one of them had died and the other found it impossible to provide the sort of home that was needed. It also might mean (and in very many cases does mean) that the biological parents of the child were not married—that the child was, as the saying goes, "born out of wedlock." ("Wedlock" means "marriage bond," or the mutual pledge that married people make to each other.) In such situations a decision might be made (usually by the mother who gave birth) that the child would have a better life in an established family. In some cases—nobody has any idea of the real number—the child's parents simply do not want a child.

Whatever the reason for the child's being left without the protection that everyone must have during childhood years, societies have always recognized the need to provide that protection. There is evidence of that recognition in the oldest set of laws that scholars have been able to find in our world. It is known as the Code of Hammurabi, and it was carved on a slab of black rock centuries ago and not discovered until 1901.

The
almost
the six
in sou
Hamn
joyed
munit
a well
most i
fact tl
regul:
them-
order,
serve
Th

and rear him as a son, the gro
be demanded back" by his b
Inheritance, or the proc
sessions, and land are
eration of a family
matter of great in
societies. But h
family if a
found the
offspri
the
t

the Code, and they dealt with most of the matters that might be expected to affect a government and its people, including questions concerning marriage, debts, crime, finance, and slavery. But at its very beginning the Code set forth the reasons Hammurabi had written it. He had done so, the Code stated, so that "the strong oppress not the weak, that the orphan and widow be protected."

Among the laws were several specific provisions for the protection of those young persons who, for whatever reason, did not have parents. One of the rules made it very clear that the Babylonians felt four thousand years ago (as society's lawmakers feel today) that once an adoption takes place, it is final and cannot be reversed. "If a man takes a child in his name," stated the Code, and if he should "adopt

wn-up son may not
iological parents.

ess by which money, pos-
passed from the older gen-
o a younger one, has been a
mportance in most of the world's
ow would such wealth be kept in the
 couple had no children—if they had
mselves unable to bear children, or if their
ng had died? One answer that occurred to
ancient Greeks and Romans, and to societies
at followed them, was adoption. It provided childless couples with the equivalent of instant heirs and,
at the same time, provided homeless children with
instant families. In some religions of the Far East,
the worship of one's ancestors is very important.
Adoption filled a need here, too, by providing
younger generations to worship their older, adoptive ancestors. These younger generations, of course,
would someday become someone else's ancestors.

You may have noticed that these attitudes toward
adoption did not always seem to be based entirely
on concern for the child who was lacking a family.
Adopting a child had certain advantages for others,
too. It not only made it possible for an otherwise
childless family to hand down its land, houses, sav-
ings account, and name through the generations;
it also made it possible for some families to exist in
the first place. And if there is one general statement
that can be made about the societies and civilizations
that have populated Earth since human life began

here, it is that great emphasis has always been placed on the value of the *family.*

It is the family group that has served through the centuries to gather food, build shelter, offer mutual protection, and assist the younger members of society in becoming grown-ups. Where a complete family could not grow all by itself—that is, where children were not born to the wife and husband—adoption has always been a handy substitute. So adoption has been an important help to society in assuring the continuity of the family.

Adoptees were helpful within the family as well. Sometimes, in fact, it became difficult to tell the difference between an adopted child and a servant. When the United States was first being settled by whites, orphans from England were sent here in considerable numbers to be adopted by families who wanted not only children to love but also extra hands to chop wood, till the soil, and fight Indians. At the end of the last century, in the 1890s, there were "orphan trains": Some ninety thousand orphans, who otherwise would have lived in dismal institutions or would have been left to fend for themselves on the streets, were put in railroad cars and shipped to towns in the Midwest.

When a train arrived in a particular town, its human cargo was unloaded and put on exhibition in churches and other meeting places. Local people who needed extra family members could come and view them and, possibly, pick out one or two, adopt them, and take them home. During the exhibitions,

the orphans were put on raised platforms so everyone could see them. Thus they were literally "put
up for adoption." This is a phrase that persisted in
our language until fairly recently. (Nowadays no
reasonably sensitive person would say someone was
"put up for adoption," because the phrase sounds
a bit cold and heartless. The phrase that's being
used now to describe the finding of an adoptive
home for a child is "being placed for adoption.")
Although some of the methods and language that
were used back in those days may seem crude to us
now, it should be remembered that an awful lot of
people were made happy, and had their lives
changed for the better, through the adoptive process. A family that adopted a child partly because
it needed more help in running a Nebraska farm
was just as capable as any other family of establish-
ing a loving, caring relationship with that child.

Three

Adoption Has Changed

Until just a few decades ago, much of the talk and effort about adoption had to do with finding the "proper" child for the family, and not the other way around. Often the agencies that specialized in introducing children who were in need of homes to parents who were in need of children would be very careful to match up physical characteristics, so that the child would look like a "real" member of the family. If the husband and wife who wanted to adopt were blond-haired and blue-eyed, the agency looked around for a blond-haired, blue-eyed baby for them. Of course, there's nothing wrong with blond-haired parents having blond-haired kids, even if the kids are adopted; but often this sort of matching was done to help *disguise* the fact that the child was adopted—to hide the fact from the rest of the world and, sometimes, even from the child him- or herself. (Yes, from the child, too. There was a time, and it wasn't all that long ago, when some experts on adoption were advising adoptive parents

11

never to tell their children that they were adopted. There'll be more about this later.) That sort of disguising was terribly short-sighted, for a couple of reasons. For one thing, it seemed to be like saying that there was something wrong with adoption; otherwise, why would someone want to hide it? And it also tended to overlook the fact that people, being as naturally inquisitive as they are, are usually pretty good at seeing through deceptions such as that one.

But the tendency to think of adoption as a service that society was offering, not for the child but for the prospective parents, continued for a long time. Some homes for children who were awaiting adoption even went so far as to publish *catalogues* that described the sort of kids they had for adoption and explained how to get one of them. Looking through these brochures wasn't exactly like glancing through the Sears, Roebuck catalogue, but it was close. Some of them even had pictures of the children.

One of those catalogues, issued back in the first quarter of this century by the Willows Nursery of Kansas City, Missouri, is almost a collector's item. Babies came to the Willows in a fairly normal way (although it was one that few people, in those days, discussed in public conversation): the out-of-wedlock route. Young women who were not married had become pregnant. They went to the Willows, or to other places like it in various sections of the country, to spend the last part of their nine-month pregnancy in an environment that was clean and fairly sympathetic and, most of all, private. Their absence from home might be explained by saying they were "away at school," or "traveling in Europe." When their babies were born, the young women turned them over to the nursery, which then had little difficulty in finding couples who were eager to adopt them. The young women returned to their homes and their former lives, confident that their babies would receive the best possible care and that their "terrible secrets" would remain secrets.

Those babies, said the Willows catalogue, were "accidents of fate," and "children of unfortunate parentage," who nevertheless were of "exceptionally high grade," and "fit to grace any home in this country that is open to a child." Explained the catalogue: "These children, born as they usually are from clean American stock, mostly from the rural districts of the Central West, although more or less are from all over the United States, make far more creditable members of a family than the legitimate child born in the poverty and vice of a congested city." (It was fashionable in those days to blame most of the world's problems on cities and the people who inhabited them.) As for the advantages of having a child from the Willows, said the publication, it was obvious that children had a beneficial effect on a marriage. "The childless home is abnormal and unsatisfying," said the catalogue. "Its tendency is toward degeneracy and dissolution of home ties and too often ends in divorce."

Hardly anybody would use such words today, but

back then plenty of people did. In fact, it was not until relatively recently—around the nineteen fifties—that American society really recognized that the important thing about adoption was not to provide a "high grade" child for every family that wanted one, but rather to provide a high grade family for every child who needed it. What was paramount, decided the professionals in the social work agencies that studied and worked on adoption issues, was the "best interests of the child." An important leader in all this was the Child Welfare League of America, which was founded in 1920 as a "children's advocate"—that is, an organization that sticks up for kids. The League's sole purpose, its leaders say, is to "improve services for children and their families." The League is very active in the adoption field, and people with an interest in the subject look to it for information and guidance.

Even more recently, starting around the nineteen seventies, adoption underwent another change. Until that time, the children who were most likely to be adopted shared three major characteristics: they were white, they were healthy, and they were very young—just a few weeks or days old. This was because many of the agencies that dealt with adoptions were concerned only with white children and parents, and because most people who wanted to adopt children wanted one who could start his or her life with them as early as possible.

For a long time, the supply of children who fit these specifications was pretty much equal to the demand. But then, by the seventies, the change became noticeable. Fewer white infants were available for adoption. The reasons for this are interesting, and they have a lot to do with other trends that were going on in the nation at the time. For one thing, there were available newer forms of contraception—devices and substances that can prevent birth—so people were more able than ever before to decide whether they were going to have babies in the first place. With the ability to make that decision, it became likely that more of the babies who *were* born would be kept by the people who gave birth to them.

For another thing, it became easier (and safer, and in most cases legal) for women who were pregnant and who didn't want to have babies to end their pregnancies long before it was time for the baby to come—to have abortions. And a third reason was that more and more women who were not married, and who became pregnant, were deciding to have their babies and then to keep them after they were born.

The question of babies' being born to unmarried women is a touchy one (although it is nowhere near as touchy as it *used* to be), but it is one that everyone who is interested in adoption must face, sooner or later, for the simple reason that a very large portion of children who are adopted started out life that way. Those babies that Willows Nursery called "accidents of fate" were children who were born out of wedlock. I was born out of wedlock, and so were

a very large number of other people. If the person
who's reading this book is an adoptee, there's a
chance that you were born out of wedlock, too. It's
not the most unusual thing in the world to be born
out of wedlock.

At any rate, for all those reasons the world of
adoption underwent a change in the last several
years. The kids most people had in mind when they
talked about "adoption" suddenly weren't as available as they had been, even though there was no
noticeable decline in the number of parents who
wanted to adopt children. This trend has had a very
good effect in another direction, however: It has
forced everyone—the social agencies, the prospective parents, and society in general—to pay more
attention to other groups of children who should
have been adopted but who always seemed to lose
out to the white infants. These are the ones who
have been known as the "hard-to-place" children,
or the kids with "special problems." What people
meant when they used these terms was that these
were the ones who were discriminated against by
most of society—the ones who were black, or whose
parents were of different races, or who were from
foreign countries, or who had sicknesses or physical
or mental disabilities, or who were several years old
and who therefore weren't as cuddly as those tiny,
innocent infants. For a very long time it was quite
common for adoption agencies, both those that
were privately run and those that were operated by
the government, to treat these children as second-

class. And often when parents who were seeking adoptive children were of the same backgrounds as the "hard-to-place" children (a black couple, for example), they discovered that the agency attitudes and rules were discriminatory against *them,* too.

This situation changed rather quickly, and the change occurred fairly recently, when the supply of young, healthy, white children declined. Joan McNamara, in a book she wrote for couples who are thinking about adopting, says that "By the 1960s the emphasis had shifted from finding the perfect baby for the perfect family to locating a family with the desire and ability to raise an adopted child—a child who could be of any age, of any racial background, with any medical condition. Just when agencies were becoming more flexible and when prospective parents were responding by approaching adoption in greater numbers, the children traditionally considered 'most adoptable' became less available." (If you're interested in finding out more about Joan McNamara's book, along with other sources of information on adoption, see the For Further Reading section, pages 96–98.)

One interesting result of all this is that it's the "hard-to-place" children who're being "advertised" these days—not in the catalogues of organizations like the Willows Nursery (which is no longer in business) but in the pages of newspapers. A New York City newspaper runs a feature on "the most adoptable child of the month," with a picture of the kid and an explanation of where prospective parents can get more information. One such youngster in a recent edition was named David, a fine-looking black child who was six years old and who, according to the paper, was "enrolled in kindergarten and enjoys it very much."

There is no reason on earth, of course, why children such as David shouldn't have a chance at a warm, loving home, too, but it looked for a long time as if they would always get the short end of the adoption stick. The lack of cuddly white infants, though, is focusing more and more attention on the "hard-to-place," and parents who want to adopt children find themselves more than ever facing the question of bringing home someone who is a little less than what they'd considered perfect—which is only right, since nobody has been found yet, adopted or nonadopted, who *is* perfect.

At the same time all of this is going on, there are other developments. People are talking more openly about adoption now than ever before. It's not nearly the mysterious subject it was when I was younger. Parents who want to adopt are probably doing a better job than ever of looking at their own feelings about adoption, and of understanding that adoption is for the benefit of the child, not just for the adopting family. People who were adopted are learning, as they grow older, that adoptees have a lot in common with each other—and that one of those things is a curiosity about their biological parents. That curiosity has not always been encouraged by the rest of society, and in fact adoptees often have felt guilty about having such perfectly normal thoughts. For some who are curious, the curiosity has led, when the adoptees are grown up, to a real search for their biological parents. But most of all, what has happened recently has been the discovery that adoption and the experience of being adopted are perfectly valid subjects for discussion—that there is absolutely no reason why anyone should feel *ashamed* of being adopted or of being an adoptive parent. Adoption is an especially valid subject for discussion between the child and his or her adoptive parents, and between an adoptee and another adoptee.

Not only is there no reason to be ashamed of being adopted; adoptees even have some of their own they can look up to. Moses, who recorded the Ten Commandments, and who therefore may be described as the most celebrated lawmaker in the history of the world, was adopted. (Remember how he was found, floating in an ark in the bulrushes, by the daughter of an Egyptian pharoah?) Superman was adopted. (Remember his parents' sending him to Earth from the doomed planet Krypton?) Beyond that, it's difficult to come up with the names of many other famous adoptees. That's not because there aren't any, but rather because for most people who were adopted, there's little reason for the rest of the world to think of them as "adoptees."

Being adopted, of course, adds something to one's life that can never be erased or forgotten. It's a part of you, in the same way being left-handed or right-handed, or being Irish or Mexican-American, or being male or female, are part of you. It's always there. But what's always there is not necessarily a big deal.

Being adopted is usually just as big a deal as you want to make it. You can, like some people, make it a very important part of your life, something that influences everything you say and do. Or you can see it as one of the many things—feelings, events, emotions, facts—that go into making you the unique young person you are, and the unique adult you'll be when you're a little older.

Four

The Statistics of Adoption

There is another indication that, while adoption is important to people who're involved in it, and while it has made a significant contribution to family life all over our planet and throughout our history, it is not something that you might call of *earth-shaking importance.* And that is that we don't keep much in the way of records on adoption.

Modern society seems to have a great interest in keeping *statistics* on most things. We are a very fact-hungry country. Every ten years, when the federal government takes its census and counts the population, it asks more and more questions that are designed to provide statistics—so we can tell how many bathtubs there are in the United States, and how many years each of us attended school, and how many miles we go to get to work. Other number-counters are busy checking on the size of the asparagus crop or calculating the number of hours of television that the average American watches each week, or figuring out how much

crunchy peanut butter we eat as compared to the
smooth kind.

You'd think that we would have tons of statistics
on adoption. But we don't, and that may be another
sign that adoption, while it is an important element
in our society, is not the sort of thing that attracts
a lot of attention.

Nobody really knows, for example, how many
adoptees there are in the country. We have been
told that there were 91,800 barber shops in the
United States in 1972, that there were 79,400,000
bicycle riders in 1977, and that 47,300,000 homes
had electric can openers in 1978. But nobody's quite
sure about the number of adoptees.

One reason for the lack of statistics is the fact that
adoption is regulated, in the U.S.A., by the indi-
vidual states, and they all have slightly different
ways of going about it, with the result that no one
seems able to get all the numbers together. One
estimate that gets repeated from time to time is that
there are about five million people in the United
States today (grown-up and children) who are
adopted. Another guess is that there are about half
that many adopted *children*, or around 2 percent of
the total child population of the nation. If that estimate is correct, then you could expect every group
of fifty children to contain one adoptee. (Of course,
if *you're* an adoptee, then you know there's at least
one in every group *you're* in.)

It's likely that when someone thinks of the term
"adoption," that person thinks of a child who is

placed with people who, until the adoption occurred, were total strangers to the child. Strictly
speaking, though, that procedure is used only in
the minority of adoptions. Most adoptions in the
United States involve a child's being placed directly
by her or his birth parents with their relatives or
a stepparent. A child's aunt and uncle, for example,
can take over the parents' job. Or a mother whose
husband has died or divorced can remarry, and the
new husband (the child's stepfather) can legally
adopt the child. One state that examined its adoption statistics over a forty-five-year period, ending
in 1979, discovered that about 75 percent of the
adoptions were of this kind.

In the state study, the next largest group of adoptions (19 percent) were handled by professional
agencies, such as private adoption centers, govern-
mental welfare departments, and orphanages and
children's homes run by various charitable and
religious groups. In these, which are sometimes
called "agency placements," the two sets of parents
involved never meet each other, and almost certainly they never learn each other's names. The
biological parents turn the child over to the agency,
and the agency finds the adoptive parents. In the
process, the child can stay at the agency for years,
or the stay can be a matter of just a few days.

Another form of adoption is the "independent
placements." In these, which accounted for about
5 percent of the adoptions in the state study, the
biological parents made arrangements for the

adoption directly with the adoptive parents, with no agency in the middle. Often, however, a professional person, such as a lawyer, a doctor, or a religious official, helps with the preparations.

Almost nothing is known about yet another method of adoption—one that operates outside the law. In these "black market adoptions," as they are called, people with babies and people who want babies exchange child for money. There usually is a middleman, and he usually is a lawyer, and he usually gets a portion of the money. Selling human beings is a disgusting thing, and making money off other people's sales of human beings is equally disgusting, but it does go on, in the United States and elsewhere. Nobody knows how many adoptions are carried out this way, and nobody knows how much money changes hands. But thousands of dollars are believed to be involved in each black market sale.

With the exception of these few statistics, very little is known about adoption and adoptees that is of a solid, scientific nature. We know that, according to a federal study in the early 1970s, most of the children who were adopted by people who were not their relatives were adopted as infants. (The state survey said that 38 percent were under one month of age when they were adopted. Another 46 percent were from one to eleven months old, while the rest were a year old or older.)

We know that the total number of adoptions in the United States started declining in the early 1970s, and we believe that a major reason is that more unmarried women who have babies are deciding to keep them.

There is research that shows that the more years of education or the more income that couples have, the more likely they are to consider adoption as a way to form a family. And adoptive parents tend to be several years older than biological parents. The likely reason for this is that adoptive couples have tried for several years to conceive children before they realized they weren't able to. When people who are infertile decide to adopt children, that doesn't necessarily mean that the adoptees are somehow their second choices. What it means, more than anything else, is that the parents were very interested in having children and in making their families complete.

There's one last statistic that demonstrates the feelings that adoptive parents have toward their new families. Scientists looked over much of the research that had been done on adoption and adoptees and found that about 78 percent of the adoptions that were studied could be called "successful." Another 8 percent, they said, were "fairly successful," and the remaining 14 percent could be called "unsatisfactory" or "poor." That's a pretty high rate of success for adoptees and their parents. It's probably not very different from the rate of success in families as a whole—families that are made up of nonadoptees as well as adoptees.

Five

Some Definitions

Before we go much further, it might be helpful to discuss a few definitions.

Everybody seems to have a clear understanding of what an "adopted child" or "adoptee" is, but there is more confusion over what to call the parents who're involved in adoption. (Remember, there are two sets of parents here.) You've seen the term "adoptive parents" a lot in this book, and will see it a lot more, but in normal conversation the term is used very little, if at all. Really, you need to say "adoptive parents" only on those occasions when you have to make sure that your listener understands you're not talking about your biological parents—and such occasions don't arise all that often.

For the rest of the time, just "parents" seems to be the best choice of word. Your *parents* are the people who help you through the early years of your life—who feed and clothe and shelter and nurture you and comfort you and hold your hand when you're sick and stick by you when you're in trouble and celebrate with you when you're happy and (it must be remembered) punish you when you misbehave. And for practically all adopted kids, these people are the adoptive parents.

There is a big lack of agreement over what to call the other set of parents, the ones who actually brought you into the world. You may have noticed that the term "biological parents" has been employed in this book. That is one of the terms that is often used. Another one that seems particularly popular right now is "birth parents." One expert has suggested the use of "bioparents," but that sounds to me a little strange, like something Mr. Spock would say on "Star Trek." Some people refer to their "first parents." There seems to be agreement that the terms "true parents," "real parents," and "natural parents" are not very good ones, because they're not really accurate. Who could be "truer" or more "real" than the parents who stayed up all night with you when you had the flu? And who would be cruel enough to refer to his adoptive parents as "unnatural?" (Of course, all kids pin titles that are a lot nastier than "unnatural" on their parents when they're angry at them, but that's a different matter.)

A term that is often misused by those who don't understand much about adoption is "foster." This term (which had its origins long ago in the word for "food") is used with other words ("foster parents," "foster home") to describe a situation in which a child without a family is assigned by a government or private agency to a private home for a temporary stay—often until an adoption can be arranged. Foster parents, then, serve very valuable functions, but they are not the same as adoptive parents. Foster parents can *become* adoptive parents, however, by going through the normal adoptive process. I know someone who started out life as an infant in a foster home, waiting to be adopted. His foster parents became so attached to the baby that they didn't want to let him go. So they made an application to adopt him. (They were familiar with the process, since they already had one adopted child.) The agency approved the adoption, and that is how I got my younger brother.

One more comment on language in this book: You may have noticed that sometimes the book refers to adoptees as "him or her" or "her or him" or just "him" or just "her." The children who are being talked about, of course, can be either male or female, unless there's some explanation to the contrary.

Six

Old and New Honesties

All that talk about what might be called the "language of adoption" started in fairly recent years. There was once a time—not really all that long ago—when there was practically *nothing* that could be called the "language of adoption." People just didn't discuss it very much. It wasn't exactly that the people who were adopted and the people who adopted them were ashamed of the subject. It was more a matter of being a bit uncomfortable with the idea.

We have touched before on some of the reasons for this. One had to do with the fact that many parents who adopt do it because they are infertile, and that has never been a subject that was easy to discuss. Although we know, in our minds, that infertility is a simple, understandable fact of human life, our feelings about it sometimes cause us trouble at other, more emotional levels. Another reason that people were uncomfortable about discussing adoption was that many, many adopted children were born out of wedlock.

Now, neither of those two reasons would have assumed the importance that they did if it hadn't been for a segment of society that we all know about: the people who snoop, snicker, gossip, pry, make fun of, and in general display an obnoxious interest in the elements of other people's lives that are really none of their business. Particularly, those elements that have to do with sex. It was just that sort of people who made a lot of adoptees and adopters decide they'd just as soon not talk about adoption very much.

And then, just a couple of decades ago, an un-expected and quite nice thing happened: People started becoming more open and less hung up about some of the things they'd previously treated with such secrecy. People started acknowledging to others (and to themselves) that sex and the creation of babies were real and important parts of life (in fact, there'd be no creatures on earth without them), and that snickering about these things was really dumb.

This was all part of what some people have called a "new honesty" about people's dealings with each other. It extended not only to matters of sex and baby-making, but to practically all the other corners of our lives—our music, our clothing, our careers, our respect for the environment. It may seem strange that at the same time this "new honesty" was being talked about so much, the United States was going through some troubles that had a lot to do with *dis*honesty—the war in Vietnam, with all the anguish it caused people here at home as well as across the Pacific, was one of those, and another was the discovery that some of the highest elected and appointed officials in the nation were lawbreakers. But really, those events contributed to the "new honesty" rather than detracted from it. They made it clearer than ever before (to anyone who paid attention) that dishonesty was very harmful to all of us and that honesty was the only policy that really worked.

So what did all of this have to do with adoption? It had a lot to do with it, because it helped the people who were involved with adoption—particularly the professional people who worked in the social agencies, and who therefore made most of the rules and policies—to realize that some of the rules and policies of the past just didn't fit in very well with the new feeling of honesty.

Take, for example, the matter of explaining to the adoptee that he or she is adopted.

Some experts used to advise adoptive parents not to tell their children that they were adopted at all. But most of the experts realized that it was proper and helpful for the child to know. Unfortunately, what the child was told often turned out to be not really the truth. Some of the experts suggested that the parents make up a little story about the child's beginnings, and they suggested that the little story be designed to make the child feel as good as possible about him- or herself, about his biological parents, and about his adoptive parents. What this often amounted to was a story that was pretty far from the truth. The *purpose* behind the little story may have been a good and worthy one, but it was not honest. It's amazing how many kids could sense that they either weren't being told all the truth or that they were being told something that wasn't the truth at all.

Often one result of such a well-meaning story was to make the child feel *bad* rather than good. That happened to me when I was seven or eight years old and expressed curiosity about being adopted. I had been informed earlier just that I was adopted; now I wanted some details.

This time I was told (by an aunt) that my parents had both been college professors, and that they had been married to each other, but that they were at the beginning of their careers and wanted to know more about the world. They wanted to do a lot of traveling. So when I was born, the story went, they placed me for adoption so that I could have a good family life and they could continue with their traveling.

The story was supposed to make me feel proud of my biological parents, and to reassure me about them and about myself, and to help me understand why they had decided to place me for adoption. But one other result, I remember very clearly, was to make me angry at them. How selfish it was, I felt, for them to be more interested in traveling than in me, their newborn son. The anger and hurt didn't last very long, however, because the more I thought about it, the more I realized that the story couldn't possibly be true. Finally, many years later, I was told a totally different story that sounded a lot more truthful. I'll talk about that a little later.

Many adoptees have been told that, shortly after they were born, their biological parents died, even when that was not really the case. And many, many adopted people have been told that their adoptive parents *chose them especially* from a roomful of babies, almost as if they had been shopping for an automobile or a television set. That story was supposed to make adoptees feel truly wanted, but it sometimes had another result: It made them wonder why, if they were all that attractive, they had been made available for adoption in the first place. And another problem with what has come to be called the "chosen baby" story is that adoptees who hear it may start to fear, even without knowing it, that they won't be able to live up to their parents' high expectations—that if they were *chosen especially,* then their new parents will be very disappointed if they turn out to be just ordinary kids instead of celebrities and geniuses. Some kids even wonder if, in the event they don't live up to the expectations, their parents might return them to that roomful of babies—a scary thing to wonder about indeed.

Of course, there's nothing at all wrong with telling an adopted child those "chosen baby" stories if they're true. But in most cases, the circumstances that led to a child's being adopted are far less dramatic, much more like the sort of thing that happens in the real world. If you happen to be one of those who *was* told a story that turned out to be a bit exaggerated, remember that your parents almost certainly wanted to help and protect you as much as they could. Many times the adoptive parents themselves were given very little information about their children's biological parents, and yet they recognized their children's need for information, and so they just did the best they could. It's very unlikely that *any* of these stories was ever told out of any but the best motives.

Fortunately for everybody, the trend these days is away from fiction and toward as much honesty as possible. The adoption experts and researchers tend to agree that the agencies should provide adoptive parents with a good deal of basic information about the nature of the child's birth, such as the biological parents' age, occupations, ethnic and social backgrounds, marriage status, and the reason for placing the child for adoption. These experts assume that the adoptive parents will use their best judgment in sharing this information with their adopted children, just as parents are expected to be as wise as possible in explaining any other of the very important facts of life.

Most of the experts also agree that it would not be best for the adoptive parents to shower *all* this information on the child at a very early age. Instead, they say, the parents should be able to supply information as the growing child needs it and is able to absorb it. It might be enough for a five year old to learn just that she was adopted; later on, as she developed a normal interest in her ethnic background, her parents would be able to supply *that*. Even later, it might be wise to explain why the child needed to be adopted.

The "new honesty," as it applies to the adoptee and the people around him, means more than a truthful explanation of how he got onto this earth. It means, also, being honest about facing up to the issues that are peculiar to adoption.

In the same sense that we understand now that sex and baby-making are proper subjects for conversation, without all the snickering and eye-rolling that went on before, we are now well on the way to accepting the fact that it's okay to talk about adoption and about being adopted. It's okay for adoptees to talk about it with each other, and it's okay to talk about it with our parents. It's okay to discuss all the things about being adopted that sometimes worry us and that sometimes leave us confused. In fact, it's more than okay. It's *healthy* to talk about these things.

What kind of things? Things like whether it's right or wrong to wonder sometimes who our biological parents were, and what they were like, and why they had to give us up. For a long time (and for *all* the time when I was growing up, in the nineteen-forties and nineteen-fifties), a lot of people who had been adopted felt somehow that they should be *guilty* when they wondered about things like that. The feeling was that you somehow weren't being fair to your adoptive parents if you wondered such things—that you would hurt their feelings if you asked questions. And so adoptees back then hardly ever talked out loud about those questions, and they tried even to keep from thinking about them.

Just as we've dramatically increased our knowledge in the last several decades about such topics as space travel, and health, and the environment, we've also learned a lot about human nature, and we now know that such thoughts are perfectly normal ones, and that there's no reason at all to feel guilty about having them. And we know a lot more about the issues of adoption and the ways they affect the people who are involved in adoption—the biological parents, the adoptive parents, and the adoptees themselves. The "new honesty" is very beneficial, then, to the adoptee and his or her parents. Right now, in fact, is the best possible time in our history to be an adopted person, because right now we are recognizing the need for openness and honesty as never before. (There hardly ever has been a *bad* time to be adopted, since growing up with a family is always a lot more fun than growing up without one.)

Seven

Some of the Differences

Children who are not adopted sometimes have a fantasy, a kind of imaginative daydream, when they are particularly angry at something that their parents have or have not done. It goes like this: The parents refuse some request the child has made, or they send him to his room to punish him for some violation of the rules. (In other words, they behave the way parents *have* to behave every once in a while if they're going to keep on calling themselves parents.) And the child says to himself, in his anger: "Those couldn't possibly be my *real* parents. My *real* parents wouldn't treat me so badly. I must be adopted!"

If you're adopted, you'll find that it's difficult to have a fantasy like that, because you *know* you're adopted. You *know* that the people who said you couldn't ride your bicycle, or who sent you to your room, or said no television for a week, are not your biological parents.

So there are some differences between adoptees and other kids. Being adopted does make people different from those who aren't adopted. None of those differences are, by their nature, bad ones. Like most of the characteristics that make one person different from all other persons, the differences are negative ones only if people choose to make them so. There is a great deal of variety in the world, thank goodness, and being adopted contributes to that variety.

It might be helpful if we took a look at some of the differences, or possible differences, that an adopted person might wonder about. Keep in mind the fact that a lot of people don't ask these questions at all, and that there's nothing wrong with *that,* either.

How do I talk with my parents about being adopted?

Theoretically one's parents should be the *easiest* people to talk to about adoption, since they're the ones who adopted you. They've been through the process just as you have, and they went through it *with* you. But many adopted persons—and many adoptive parents—find it difficult to talk at all about this most important subject.

Remember, both of you are trying to protect the other's feelings. And both of you are probably a little confused about what's the "best" way to discuss adoption. Not even the people who think of themselves as experts know very much about this. It's that sort of confusion, and resulting hesitation, that sometimes causes problems and hurt feelings. Clearly, everything we know now about human nature points to the idea that talking about things like this is beneficial—and that not talking, and keeping our confusions and worries to ourselves, is likely to be harmful. It's amazing how much better you can feel simply by talking your problems over with someone else who's a sympathetic listener. If you have questions about adoption in general, about what you were like when you were little, about what is known of your biological parents, and about your adoptive parents' feelings about your adoption, by all means ask them. Your parents may not know all the answers, and they may be a little flustered at first, but when they decided to become parents they signed on as question-answerers as well.

At the same time, it doesn't hurt for you to remember that talking about adoption will probably make your parents a little nervous and confused, too. Free and open discussion about adoption is something that is only now becoming popular, and parents haven't had much education as to how to discuss the subject with their children. It just might be that your parents are waiting for *you* to raise the subject. One child welfare group, the Association for Jewish Children of Philadelphia, started a program a few years ago that enables adoptive parents to come in and talk about the things that are bothering them. In a report on the program, Shirley Sagin said that at first, "Parents were bewildered about how to communicate with the child who asked no questions." And the parents worried, too, about when to explain to their children that they were adopted and about how much to explain. Most of all, the parents in the meetings seemed to want very badly to do the right thing in communicating with their children, but they were quite uncertain about what the "right thing" was.

One thing that you might want to remember in your dealings with your parents is that, although the "chosen child" explanation of adoption has been put down by some people as possibly harmful story-telling, it's also partly true. Your adoptive parents really *did* deliberately set out to make a home for a child, and they really *did* welcome you into that home.

The births of a lot of people on this planet were not carefully planned. It's quite likely that the births of many, if not most, adopted kids were "acciden-tal," as the saying goes. But there's no doubt at all that the child's entry into the adoptive home is not only a well-planned, but also a very exciting and welcome event. Few people have such good, solid evidence that they are wanted as do adopted children.

And what about that *other* set of parents that every adoptee has, or has had? Is it "normal" to wonder about them?

Of course it is. How could you not be interested in the people who brought you into the world—especially when the conditions of your life are such that you don't know them, don't know very much about them, and when they're in general a mystery to you?

In years past, of course, the rule on all sides was to talk as little as possible about an adoptee's biological parents—to act as if they didn't exist and never did. Adoptive parents were advised to never bring up the subject of birth parents, and when their children asked questions, the rule was to say as little as possible. Adopted children, like all other children, are sensitive to all that goes on around them—to not only what is discussed, but to what *isn't* discussed as well—and so they learned not to bring up the matter at all.

None of this, though, removed the questions that practically every adopted person must ask, at some point or another, and that many people maintain are the most basic questions of the adoptee's life: *What were my biological parents like, and why did they give me up?*

Now that society is closer to understanding that these are very sensible, reasonable questions, and that it would be unusual if adoptees *didn't* ask them, they are questions that are becoming much easier to ask.

With our growing understanding of the nature of adoption, the agencies and experts are starting to share more information about the biological parents with the adoptive parents. And adoptive parents who truly want to help their children understand the experience of being adopted are realizing that, when the child is ready for it, they must share that information with him. Usually that information does not include the names of the biological parents, but it includes a lot more that the child eventually wants and needs to know. In this era of ethnic pride, for example, it's almost essential to know if you're Irish, or Polish, or Lithuanian, or Jamaican, or whatever. For some people, religious heritage is just as important. (And, in the old days, it could be very confusing. New York City is a place where people have a lot of ethnic and religious consciousness. Some adoption agencies in New York used to assign kids their religion according to the day of the week they came to the agency. If it was Tuesday, you grew up Jewish, if it was Wednesday you were Catholic, and if it was Thursday you must be Protestant.)

And the adoptee is now more likely than ever to expect an honest answer to the question, *Why did they give me up?*

Sometimes that very central question is phrased differently: *Why did they give me away?* But that's not quite accurate, since you can give *away* only something you own, and people can't own other people. Nevertheless, a lot of adopted people seem to talk about being *given away*. It's not hard to see that they're expressing a kind of hurt, a feeling of resentment, against their biological parents for doing what they did. They may be thinking (even without knowing it): *Even though I don't know why they did it, there's no reason good enough for them to have given me up. They treated me just like an object they didn't want any longer. They gave me away.*

Since we know that most kids were able to see through the fancy stories of the past (those tales about biological parents who were killed in airplane crashes, but who were in no pain before they died; and, in my case, about college professors who felt a great need to travel), and since we know now that honesty really is the best policy, the adoptee is more likely than ever to get a straight story. And the straight story is likely to be a lot less dramatic than the made-up ones, and a lot easier to understand and to sympathize with. When the adoptee knows the real reason, he may understand why he was *given up*—and he may understand that he was not really *given away* at all.

Three social scientists in California have studied adoption, adoptees, adoptive and biological parents thoroughly in recent years. They are Arthur D. Sorosky, a psychiatrist; Annette Baran, a psychotherapist; and, Reuben Pannor, a social worker. Together they have published a great deal of information about their research. Much of it is summarized in a book, *The Adoption Triangle*, which would be good reading for any young person in the late teens who wants to know more about adoption. In their discussion of information they have collected on biological parents, the authors reported the reasons those parents had given for placing children for adoption.

They included the fact that the mother was not

married; a young mother's need to finish school; financial problems; a feeling of not being ready to be a proper parent; and pressures from others to give up the baby.

In other words, the reasons all seem real and honest, and not overwhelmingly mysterious or selfish ones at all. Most birth parents, apparently, have the baby's interests at heart. They feel that he or she would have a better chance at succeeding in life if that life starts out in an adoptive home.

The California researchers found, also, that biological parents were concerned, after they had given the children up, that the children might not understand that they were trying to do the right thing. "Feelings of loss, pain, and mourning continued to be felt by the majority of birth parents" who were studied, wrote the authors, "years after the relinquishment. An overwhelming majority experienced feelings of wanting the children to know they still cared about them and expressed an interest in knowing what kind of persons their children had grown up to be."

Obviously, then, there's a lot of evidence that an adopted child is a loved child and a wanted child. His adoptive parents showed their love when they adopted him, and they show it throughout their lives afterward. From what we know, his biological parents continue to wish him a good life long after they have placed him for adoption. And, for young adoptees, there is further evidence as well: In recent years, as we noted before, it has become very easy for someone who didn't want to have a baby to avoid having one, either by preventing conception in the first place or by terminating the pregnancy. The fact that a baby is born these days is pretty nearly solid proof that someone wanted that baby to live, to be loved, and to have the best possible life.

Eight

Another Question

Suppose I'm illegitimate?

First of all, you aren't. "Illegitimate" means "not legitimate," which means "not legal." And anyone who's adopted is legal. You have all the rank and privileges of family membership, and you're just as legitimate as anyone else in the world.

The term "illegitimate" came from an era when the lack of a legally recognizable father meant that someone could not claim inheritance or enjoy the other family legal rights. Another term for someone with this status, or lack of it, was "bastard." They mean the same thing, but you're more likely to hear "bastard" these days because the term has taken on a quite different meaning. It has become a vulgar expression, used to describe someone who's mean, nasty, and offensive.

Back in our civilization's earlier days, there was no stigma, or negative meaning, attached to either word. Under early Roman law, bastards had a clearly defined status under the law. When a bastard was born in, or almost in, a royal family (which was something that happened quite frequently), she or he was given special privileges. One of the Kings of England was named William the Conqueror and, because his parents weren't married, he also was called William the Bastard, and nobody seemed to care terribly much about his background. Later on, in what has been referred to as the Puritan era, people became much more nosy about other people's moral lives, and illegitimacy took on a decidedly negative meaning. Much of society looked down on illegitimate people, in much the same way that they looked down on poor people.

Nowadays, people who have respect for language and others' feelings use neither the term "bastard" not the term "illegitimate" to describe someone whose parents were not married. Rather, they use the somewhat cumbersome term we discussed before: "born out of wedlock."

Being born in that fashion is not at all unusual today, and the stigma that is associated with it seems to be gradually slipping away as more and more unmarried mothers decide to keep and raise their babies. One estimate by a population expert for the federal government is that in one time period for which good statistics were kept, the years 1957 through 1974, there were 68,353,000 people born in the United States. Of that total, 5,516,100 of the births were out of wedlock. So about 8 percent of all the births in the nation were out of wedlock. If, just for the fun of it, we rather unscientifically applied that percentage to the population of the nation as a whole in 1980, which was the last time we counted ourselves, that would be about eighteen million people, or more folks than presently live in Arizona, Colorado, Georgia, Idaho, Indiana, and Maine, combined.

So it's easy to see that being "illegitimate" is not all that unusual. And remember: If you're adopted, you're just as "legitimate" as anyone else. As for being a "bastard," that would apply only if you're mean, nasty, and offensive—qualities that can apply to adoptees and nonadoptees alike.

Nine

Nature and Nurture

Am I the person I am because of my biological parents or because of my adoptive parents?

A big controversy has been going on for a very long time in the sciences—both the "hard" sciences of chemistry and biology and the like, and the "human" sciences of psychology and similar fields—over the question of heredity versus environment. Sometimes it's called "nature versus nurture." The question is: Which is more important—which has more influence over the way a person develops—that person's basic, hereditary makeup (over which the person and those around her have very little control) or the environment in which the person lives (over which lots of people have lots of control)?

If we knew the answer to this, we'd know the answer to a lot of questions about why people behave the way they do. And we'd be able to know just how much of an adopted person's behavior, good or bad, is the way it is because it was inherited that way, or how much of it comes from the environment that's provided by the adoptive parents.

(Sometimes adoptive parents think they know the answer to this question. When their children act in ways that completely baffle them, they wring their hands and conclude that the behavior *must* have been inherited from the "other" set of parents.)

If heredity, or "nature," were the big, important, controlling factor in the lives of adoptees, then the most important part of those lives would be the part the adoptees know little or nothing about—the part that was contributed by the biological parents. Then it would be easy to understand that adoptees had an overwhelming need, whether they understood it or not, to know more about that part of their lives.

If, on the other hand, it was environment, or "nurture," that was important, then the part played by the biological parents wouldn't be very important at all. The environment provided by the adoptive parents would be all-important.

The argument over heredity versus environment is an old one, and it threatens to go on forever. People who believe one side of it are just as passionate as the believers on the other side. And when the controversy is applied to adoption, there are plenty of arguments on both sides.

The brother of an adoptee wrote not long ago, in a publication for adopted people, that "It is incredible to see how indestructible heredity is, and I suspect it plays a much bigger part than I ever imagined. . . . You are what you are born, way down deep." For him, heredity was all-important.

The catalogue of the Willows Nursery, the place that referred in the 1920s to adoptees as "accidents of fate," argued that heredity was *not* all that important. In fact, it discussed adoptees almost as if they were lumps of modeling clay, ready to be run through a Pla-Doh Fun Factory and turned by their new environment into whatever sorts of people their new parents wanted: "Given an average child and place it at birth under the proper surroundings," said the catalogue, and "practically anything may be done with it. It may be developed in almost any direction. Probably not more than 10 percent of its future would be due to its heredity. The remaining 90 percent is due to the environment—the home, school, church, and community into which the child is thrown."

So what's the answer? Is it environment or heredity? Nature or nurture?

The answer, of course, at least as far as we have been able to determine with the information we now have, is *both*. Some of our characteristics are inherited. These include the color of our hair and eyes, the tendency toward certain kinds of diseases and medical conditions, such as muscular dystrophy and diabetes and nearsightedness. Some *other* of our characteristics are influenced by our environment. We may develop a particular interest in a subject at school, and the reason may be not an inherited talent for biology, but rather an especially skillful, caring teacher. Certain lung diseases that are suffered by coal miners and workers in textile mills appear to be totally influenced by the environments in which they work. But many other characteristics—perhaps most—seem to be the results of combining heredity and environment. We may have inherited a tendency toward certain kinds of heart trouble, for instance, but the sort of food we eat and the kind of lives we live may play an equal part in the conditions of our hearts. A tendency for lung diseases may be inherited, but cigarette smoking may have just as much to do with the health, or lack of health, of our lungs.

What we are, and what we will be when we get older, is really the result of a *mixture* of hereditary and environmental factors, and scientists have not been able to demonstrate that either set of forces is consistently stronger than the other. I would argue, though, that the adoptee's environment has an edge over her or his heredity, if only for the reason that being adopted is a lot more satisfactory than the alternative, which is not being adopted, which may mean living in an institution rather than a home. And, although institutions can be operated in a warm, loving, caring way, there's absolutely no place like home.

One group of researchers who studied the long-term development of adopted children found, as might be expected, that several of the children seemed to be happier and better adjusted than the rest. Their report, published by the Child Welfare

League in 1970, was titled "A Followup Study of Adoptions (Vol. II): Post-Placement Functioning of Adopted Children." The "common ingredient" in the lives of those children, said the scientists, "seemed to be the binding tie of identification—the sense of belonging, of being valued and important in the family. It is this tie of identification which may overcome disadvantages in adoption for the family and child, and lead to a successfully functioning family." The researchers declared that the "major finding" of their work was "that the fact of adoption *per se* is not so important to the child's functioning as the quality of his life experience."

So if you get sent to the principal's office for making faces at your friends in Social Studies, you can blame it on whatever you want to, but don't blame it on some mysterious extra set of parents that you've never seen. There is no known gene for making faces at friends in Social Studies. You're responsible for that particular trait yourself.

Ten

Identity

Another question is a big one:

Do adopted kids feel and think differently about other people and about the world in general?

That isn't the same thing as wondering if adopted kids are different. We know that the experience of being adopted does make us different from those people who aren't adopted. Here the questions are: *Do I function any differently because I'm adopted? Are there differences in the ways adopted people look at life, at themselves, and at the people around them?*

Another way of putting it is, *Am I subject to particular stresses and pressures just because I'm adopted? Or, Am I subject to particular joys and happinesses because of the difference?* There are plenty of people, both experts and nonexperts, who're more than willing to offer opinions on these questions. As in the arguments over heredity and environment, there is no one single correct set of answers.

One particularly important thing to remember

as you consider this question is that you should be very skeptical about believing generalized statements about adoptees. If someone says, "All adoptees are such-and-such," or even "*Most* adoptees feel thus-and-so," you have a perfect right and duty to question those statements. Adoptees make up a very large, very diverse group of people. Some are very young, some are very old, some are your age. Some are bright, some are not-so-bright. Adoptees are pink, black, brown, other colors, male, female, plain, beautiful, fat, and skinny. Some adoptees spend a lot of time thinking about the fact that they were adopted, while some spend almost no time thinking about that fact.

There is a great variety of conditions under which people are adopted. Some enter their adoptive families as infants; some are several years old. There may be differences in the way adoptive parents handle their roles. So it's quite easy to see how being adopted might influence some kids' feelings about themselves, others, and life in general, while in others it might not make much difference at all.

What it all boils down to is the idea that adoptees, like everybody else, are very hard to describe in sweeping, all-encompassing terms. There are some characteristics that *do* seem to be found in *many* children who are adopted, but there are not many such characteristics and they certainly don't apply to everybody. Adoption, then, produces children, teenagers, and adults who're pretty much as diverse as the rest of the population. When you consider the fact that the event that begins the process of adoption is a very dramatic and traumatic one—the transfer of the child from one set of parents to another—and you consider the fact that the people who went through that event turn out to be very much like everybody else in society, you have to conclude that adoption is an all-around good deal, and that it functions with amazing smoothness.

There are some people, though, who see adoptees as people who cannot help but be "damaged" and "scarred" by the process they've gone through. It has been ordinary, and almost fashionable, for psychologists and psychiatrists and other social scientists who have had dealings with adopted persons (both as children and later on when they are grown up) to report that they have found evidence of some of these "damages" and "scars."

The 1970 report called "A Followup Study of Adoptions" also reviewed what other social scientists had said about adoptees. It concluded that adopted persons had a "greater vulnerability to stress" and to the sort of problems that might bring them to a child guidance center or a facility for the treatment of psychiatric problems than did nonadopted people. The social workers who wrote the report demonstrated their lack of sensitivity by referring to the nonadopted as "natural children"— as if adoptees were somehow "unnatural."

Another group—the California researchers, Sorosky, Baran, and Pannor—has reported that "Many adult adoptees appear to suffer from low self-esteem and at the same time to carry 'chips on their shoulders.' They seem to be angry at the world which has withheld knowledge of their birthright from them. But they also feel embarrassed about their adoptive status and view themselves as 'unfinished' or 'imperfect.' "

It very well might be that such feelings occur more often among adoptees than among those who were not adopted, or that they are more noticeable and intense when they occur in adoptees. But we have no proof of this. It should not be surprising that social workers, psychologists, and psychiatrists who deal with adoptees will recognize such feelings among their patients; in fact, similar feelings are often found among *all* sorts of people, adopted or not, who seek professional help of this sort. But it must be remembered that there are great numbers of adoptees, grownup and younger, who make their ways through life without being greatly bothered by such feelings any more than anyone else is.

And of course, a *lot* of people in this world, adoptees and nonadoptees alike, view themselves as "unfinished" and "imperfect." That is a part of the human condition. When you stop being "unfinished," you're ready for the cemetery. And I know of no one who has stopped being "imperfect." I do know a few who think they have achieved perfection, but no one who knows them agrees with that assessment.

Another researcher, Margaret Lawrence, talked with a large number of grown-up adoptees and found what she felt were similar problems. The adoptees, she reported, presented a picture of "a child struggling, alone, with overwhelming confusions and insecurities." The adoptees spoke of themselves as "isolated, insecure, lonely, usually obedient and well behaved, different—and often disturbed. They reported that they did, and still do, lack self-confidence, self-esteem, and a solid sense of identity."

That last term—the "sense of identity"—is one that pops up frequently when social scientists write and talk about adoptees.

Everyone, when she or he is growing up, goes through various stages of acquiring an *identity*—that collection of characteristics and traits and experiences that makes us individuals. Our parents are very helpful in this process. We depend on them totally at first, and then we start learning from them. They are very important in transmitting knowledge to us from the past to use in the present and the future. Later on (when, one hopes, we have learned enough), we end our dependence on our parents and set out on our own, armed with lots of information and experience and our own unique identity. The process is normal and natural and unending and it's the way we keep human life going on our planet.

Some social scientists believe that this construction of an identity is particularly difficult for an adoptee, who always knows that some of the building materials—the biological parents—are usually just not available.

The California researchers are particularly concerned about this. "The totality of adult identity," they have written, "is rooted in ties with the past, which for the adoptee does not exist, no matter how nurturing his/her legal family has been." Without a proper way to build his identity, they say, the adoptee can find himself developing "a sense of shame, embarrassment, and lowered self-esteem."

It all sounds pretty bad. If these characteristics and problems apply to all adoptees, or even to adoptees in general, then the typical adopted person is not only different from other people, but is probably mixed-up and miserable as well.

Fortunately, there is no real evidence that that is the case.

Much, probably most, of the scientific research that has been published about adoption and adoptees is based on the experiences of those adoptees who come to child guidance clinics and similar agencies. In other words, the people who are being studied have already acknowledged that they have some problems—with self-esteem, identity, or whatever. Very little of the research that has been done on adoption has been done by scientists who have tried to look at the lives of adoptees *in general*, including those adoptees who never feel a need to seek psychiatric help. There's absolutely nothing wrong with seeking help—in fact, there's everything right with it—but it is misleading to take a look at the characteristics of those adoptees who do seek help and then to make general, wide-ranging comments about *all* adoptees. Viola W. Bernard, a psychiatrist who works with children and who has for a long time had a special interest in adoption, has written: "Reports from guidance clinics, agencies, and physicians about disturbed adoptive children" cannot serve as good measures of adoption in general, "since these sources have but a one-sided view. They do not see the many well-adjusted adoptive families as well, and thus lack access to the total picture." So if you're an adoptee, and you feel pretty good about yourself, and you think your identity's coming along pretty nicely, don't worry. *You* may be the average adoptee.

There are some areas where it stands to reason that adoptees may be somewhat more sensitive. Everyone seems to agree that the adoptee's life is likely to be influenced by that very important event at the beginning of it—the fact that she or he was transferred from one set of parents to another. For some, as we have seen, the term for this is "They gave me away," and the feeling is one of rejection. That feeling can still be there even when you know very well that the "giving away" occurred for perfectly sensible reasons.

So it should not be surprising that adoptees would

be more sensitive than most people to anything in their later lives that might sound or feel like rejection or abandonment. A child who gets separated from her mother in a department store or shopping center finds herself in a very frightening situation, although it's one that hardly ever lasts long. But for the adopted child, the event may be especially terrifying because it reminds her (even in her subconscious mind) of the separation that occurred before, at birth.

It is reasonable to expect that one of the ways people who are concerned about rejection use to deal with that concern would be to avoid situations where they might be rejected. So it may be that some adoptees find themselves shying away from very close relationships with other people. The reason, which is not always a conscious one, could be that avoiding closeness is also avoiding the possibility of being rejected.

Knowing that you may be more sensitive to rejection because you're an adoptee can be helpful, though. It always is helpful when you're able to figure out what makes yourself tick, and when you're able to understand your reactions to various problems. That is part of growing up and it's part of building your identity.

Identity, by the way, is not just a matter of finding out about, and reacting with, your history. Unless you're the laziest person in the world, you're probably going to have to work for a living when you grow up. You won't live entirely off what you inherit. It's similar with your identity. Some of it comes from what you inherit, in your genes and those first few moments after birth, and even, as some scientists believe, in those nine months that you dozed in your mother's belly. But a lot of it comes from you, too. It develops with you; you build on it, grow into and out of it. You *create* your identity as you live and grow.

Some of the experts think that adoptees are lonelier than most people. But another side of that loneliness, if it exists in you, may be the exciting feeling of knowing that you, more than most people, are participating in the construction of your own identity. With the help of your adoptive parents, you're building a history. You may not be able to summon up, as some people can, the stories about your great-great-great grandfather Ezekiel who was born during the Civil War and swam across the Mississippi on a dare, or your grandmother Louisa who had a confrontation with a porcupine. But you will be able to have the satisfaction of knowing that right now you're creating your own history—your own stories that your great-great grandchildren will be telling years from now.

By the way: There are some scientific studies that conclude that adoptees are *not* really very different from anyone else—or that whatever problems they have are not the sort that cause them any more problems than anybody else.

One such study, by psychologists at Drew

University in New Jersey, found that adoptees were different from persons who were not adoptees, but that the differences were all in the adoptees' favor. Kathlyn S. Marquis and Richard A. Detweiler looked at groups of young adoptees and nonadoptees and concluded that "adopted persons feel more positive about themselves and about others," and feel "more in control and more confident than do the nonadopted persons in our sample." They added: "There is not a shred of evidence in this study that indicates any of the negative characteristics of dependency, fearfulness, tenseness, hostility, loneliness, insecurity, abnormality, inferiority, poor self-image or lack of confidence."

The important thing to remember from all this, then, is that, while the adoptee may have some of the feelings, and even anxieties, that are believed to occur more often in adoptees, the adoptee never has to be a *prisoner* of those feelings. The problems that are associated with being adopted, like the problems that are associated with anything else, can always be discussed with others—with other adoptees, with your doctor, your teacher, and particularly with your parents. The problems can almost always be worked out.

Eleven

The Grownup Adoptee

Will being adopted make me somehow different when I become older?

Some experts believe that adolescence, which is a tough time for everyone, may contain some special strains for adoptees. Adolescence is a time in which you're developing in many ways. You're becoming sexually mature, for one thing, and that always provides some tensions. Also, people who're going through adolescence may tend to wonder more, and to wonder out loud more, about their ethnic and historical background—their genealogy. This, too, may cause some tension when you realize that you just don't know much about your genealogy.

The fact that you were adopted may loom large in your mind, too, when you've become an adult and are starting a family of your own. Although social agencies are more aware now than ever before of the need to gather and collect more information about the health and medical character-

64

istics of biological parents—because the entire nation is more aware of the ways in which genetic diseases and conditions are transmitted—in the past not much information of this sort was gathered. As a result, adoptees who were about to become mothers and fathers themselves might have worried about whether their offspring would suffer from some previously unknown, genetically transmitted trait.

In the great majority of the cases, of course, anyone who did worry about such things was pleasantly relieved to find that he or she had become the parent of a normal, healthy baby. And, for adoptees who had not had any contact with their biological parents, there has always been an extra added kick: Their new daughter or son represents the first real "blood relative" they have ever known! Like all parents, I'll never forget any of the events and emotions that accompanied the birth of my own daughter. One of them (after I had counted her fingers and toes and noted that the reason she was so beautiful was that she took after her mother) was the sudden, intense realization that, biologically speaking, she was the closest kinfolk I'd ever met!

There's another possible difference that might pop up when you become an adult, and it's also in the nature of an extra added attraction: You might find that, because you were adopted, you've developed a sensitivity about families and relationships that a lot of other people don't have. You might have a better appreciation of the responsibilities and obligations that go along with starting a family. And you almost certainly will understand better than most people the emotions and sensitivities that are involved in becoming a parent. Your parents—your adoptive parents—will have taught you a lot about that.

Twelve

Suppose You're Not Curious?

Suppose being adopted doesn't make me feel different at all? Suppose I'm not curious about the things that adoptees are said to be so curious about?

Great. Fine. Wonderful. You're just as "normal" as somebody who *does* feel different and who *is* curious. Remember, there's an enormous amount of diversity in the world, among adoptees as well as among all other people. So you're not suffering from identity problems? Find it easy to communicate with your parents? None of those nagging feelings of rejection? You'll just have to think up other things to worry about. Fortunately, life contains an endless supply of them, so the only thing you can be sure you'll never have to worry about is being bored.

Thirteen

The Search for Roots

For some adoptees, though, curiosity about being adopted is a very large, important part of their personalities. They think about it a lot, and they realize that they won't be satisfied until they have learned more about the origins of their lives.

Some people refer to this as "looking for my roots." That kind of search has always been popular, of course, but the idea became *really* popular a few years ago when writer Alex Haley published a book, titled *Roots,* that was about a black American's attempts to trace his ancestry back through the era of slavery, even further into tribal Africa. Haley's book, and a television version of it that was watched by millions of people, gave a lot of folks the desire to find out more about their own "roots."

By the thousands, Americans dug out old family Bibles and other records, and they started interviewing the oldest members of their families for their recollections, and they descended on public libraries and government archives to find out more information. Some of them returned (as Haley did when he visited Africa) to the places where their forebears had lived hundreds of years ago, and they held joyful "reunions" with very distant relatives they had never known, some of whom didn't even speak their same language.

This urge to establish or reestablish ties with the past has affected adopted persons, too. Hardly anyone is not interested in her or his past. But looking for roots has been especially difficult for adoptees, if not impossible, since one of the foundations of adoption, at least as we know it in this time and in this nation, is the deliberate cutting away of roots.

The very process of adoption has included the separation of the present from the past: Those who live in the present—the adoptee and the adoptive parents—are hardly ever allowed or encouraged to see, talk with, or even to know about the people who, in their minds, reside in the past—the biological parents or their relatives. Often, when birth records are changed to give the adoptee his "new" last name, places of birth and the exact dates of birth have been changed as well, to make sure that the adoptee cannot "go back" in time to discover the past. The reason that was traditionally given for all this was quite simple: It was for the protection of the child. The people who made the rules realized that a change as deeply important to someone's life as his adoption must be a very final change, one that could not be reversed. Once the child entered his or her new life, they figured, every precaution should be taken to make sure that the new life would not be threatened.

The rule, then, was to draw a definite, uncrossable line between the adoptee and his or her biological roots. As a 1979 publication of the Juvenile Rights Project of the American Civil Liberties Union Foundation put it: "The law of adoption creates a total break in the relationship between a child and his birth parents and endows the adoptive family with all the legal attributes of a parent-child relationship, as though the adopted child were the natural child of the adoptive parents. As stated by an English judge twenty-three years ago, the law draws a 'veil' between the past and present lives of adopted persons and makes it 'as opaque and impenetrable as possible, like the veil which God has placed between the living and the dead.' "

A veil as thick as that would be pretty thick indeed. But the fact is, some adopted people have been breaking through that veil, especially in recent years. They've been seeking out and sometimes finding one or both of their biological parents, and in many cases they've been finding the answers to questions such as "What were my birth parents like?" and "Why was I placed for adoption?"

Some of these *searches*, as they are called, have turned out to have very happy endings, and some have been quite disappointing. The business of adopted people's searching has received a lot of publicity in the press and on television, and several organizations have been formed of adoptees who are searching. Efforts are being made by some of these people to change the laws so that the "veil" between past and present can be removed, or at least made less impenetrable. The searching issue is a big one—the biggest one affecting the adoption world right now—and, if you're an adoptee, you can expect it to touch on your life, sooner or later, in one way or another.

This is not the same as saying you have to take part in a search for your biological parents. It *is* saying that questions about searching will surely be put to you in the future, possibly by your friends, or by other adoptees, or your parents, or almost certainly by your own inner self.

Throughout history, some adopted people have searched for their biological parents, to be sure. But there seems to be a particular emphasis on searching right now, and it looks as if the emphasis came about as a result of several recent historical events. The movement for black people's civil rights came dramatically to the world's attention in 1954, when the United States Supreme Court ruled that school segregation was unconstitutional, and again in 1960, when young blacks held a "sit-in" in a store that had treated them unfairly. Since that time, dozens of groups of Americans, ranging from poor people to old folks to gays to people who must use wheelchairs, have gotten together and demanded that the rest of society respect their rights: They have protested laws and customs they thought were

wrong and they have argued for new laws and customs they felt would treat them better.

The same sort of changes have been occurring
among adoptees. As is the case with the other
groups, not every adoptee has demanded and protested. Some might not even feel that there is a need
for protest. But others have felt such a need, and
as a result the public in general is much more aware
of adoption than before. And one of the issues it
is aware of is the belief by some adoptees that they
should search.

Robin Peacock, who is the adoption expert for
the North Carolina Division of Social Services,
explained not long ago to a legislative commission
studying adoption that: "Starting in the mid-to-late
sixties and continuing—and increasing—through
the seventies, and resulting from a combination of
many factors, beginning with the protest move-
ments, with the emerging rights of minorities, with
generally expanding attitudes of openness and
honesty, with lessening of societal stigma toward
children born out of wedlock, and with increasing
interest in one's heritage, we have seen and heard
from adoptees who are searching for information
about their birth parents and their siblings, for any
number of reasons."

Because of all the new interest in adoption and
because of the new visibility of adoptees, there have
been changes in some of the adoption laws. Scotland
and England and Israel are among the places where
laws have changed; Minnesota is one of the United

States that has revised its rules. What the changes generally do is make information from the original birth records available to adoptees ("unsealing the birth records," it is called) under certain conditions. Usually those conditions include the requirement that an adoptee be an adult before he or she may see the records. If the biological parent does not want to be "found," that wish is honored. And often there is a requirement that before any information is passed along, the adoptee must have a discussion with an expert in the field—a "counselor"—about what he hopes to find and why he's searching.

As is the case with many aspects of adoption, we don't really know much about searching. There is very little solid information about why people search, and about why some people feel a very strong need to search and others seem to feel no need at all. We don't know whether searchers are driven by a desire to learn about their background or whether the most important thing to them is meeting their birth mother or father. We don't know what percentage of the adopted people are searching, or what percentage want to search, nor do we have any idea of the actual number of people who are searching.

We do have evidence that searching is done almost exclusively by adult adoptees, and that women seem more likely to search than men. It also looks as if it is the biological mother that most searchers try to find. These last two findings may be related to the fact that females are more closely connected with the birth process than are males.

Some of the scientists who have studied searchers and searching feel that those who do seek their biological parents are more likely to have been placed for adoption later in life than those who don't search, and to have been somewhat uncomfortable with their adoptive parents. This is not a solid scientific fact at all, however, and there are many examples to the contrary. Also, not all the searchers are the adoptees themselves. In some cases, women or men have tried to find the children they placed for adoption years before.

Fourteen

Searching: Why, When, Who

One of the scientific studies on searching was done in the late 1970s in England, shortly after that nation revised its laws to give adopted people over the age of eighteen the right to get a copy of their original birth certificate, after first meeting with a counselor. Cyril Day, himself a counselor in England's General Register Office, which keeps records and statistics, wrote a report on the study, which examined the experiences of the first five hundred applicants under the new law. In the British study, the "search" was referred to as a "trace."

The main reasons for most of the applications, wrote Day, were a need to "complete a sense of true self-identity," and, as some put it, "curiosity." The applicants came from a great variety of social and intellectual backgrounds, he wrote, yet all of them "shared one overall purpose. They wished to know, beyond all doubt, and from official records, the true verifiable facts of their origin." The study presented some other "tentative conclusions," among which were:

Fewer adoptees made applications than the officials had expected. Day said those who applied formed between 1 and 2 percent of the adopted adults affected by the new law. Far more women than men were involved. The "great majority" of those who applied "appeared to be stable and well adjusted."

It appeared to the counselors that successful adoptions were more likely to result when the adoptee was accepted into his or her new family, and when there was a feeling of "unthreatened security," along with "loving relationships based on mutual trust." (Of course, that's a pretty good recipe for successful memberships in any family, whether it's adoptive or not.)

"Applicants with an unhappy adoptive experience were much more likely to trace," wrote Day.

About one-third of the applicants said they intended to trace until they found their biological parents. Another one-third seemed satisfied with the basic written information they got from the newly unsealed birth records, and the final one-third seemed uncertain about what they would do next.

One noticeable characteristic of the British applicants, wrote Day, was "primary loyalty to the adoptive parents." The searchers seemed especially concerned that their adoptive parents not be hurt. Because of this, many of the adults were carrying on their searching without telling their adoptive parents.

Little solid information has been gathered about why some adoptees search, and about why some do not. There may be the simple, understandable feeling, which was reported by many of the adoptees in the study in England, that people had a "right to know" the details of something of such great importance.

For some, there is anger that the system of adoption, as it has evolved in this nation, has served to protect two of the sides of the "adoptive triangle" more than the other. The privacy of the biological parents is protected, say these people, and the legal rights of the adoptive parents are protected. But the law does little to assist the adoptee when she wants to know basic facts of her origin. What particularly angers these people is the fact that these laws, which they consider unjust and unconstitutional, go on penalizing the adoptee long after he becomes an adult.

For almost everyone who searches, though, the reason for the search boils down to one word: *identity*. Those who search feel that until they have undertaken their search, their identities are not complete. They would agree with a judge in Missouri who wrote in a decision on adoption: "All of us need to know our past, not only for a sense of lineage and heritage, but for a fundamental and crucial sense of our very selves: Our identity is

incomplete and our sense of self [is] retarded without a real personal historical connection. Is there
any reasonable justification for us to prevent, in
perpetuity, the genealogical self-discovery of those
among us who were adopted?"

It is important to realize, though, that *identity* has
different meanings for different people. As was
demonstrated in the study of the English adoption
law, some people feel they must find a birth parent
in order to satisfy their search for identity. Others
do not, and some haven't made up their minds yet.

There are many ways of conducting a search,
ranging from all-out sleuthing, of the sort that's
found in detective thrillers, to accidental discover-
ies. Some adoptees who have searched speak of
walking down the street, searching the faces of
everyone they see, looking for someone who "looks
like me." Some searchers have found their biological parents after searches that lasted two weeks,
and others have looked for twenty years. Sometimes
the people who keep the records—at adoption
agencies or at state archives, where birth, death,
health, and population documents are kept—hand
over information to an adult adoptee who asks for
it, even though the law does not allow them to do
so. Some adoptees have gone into court to try to
convince a judge that there is a reasonable need for
their sealed record to be unsealed. Often the reason
given for such action is that the adoptee needs to
obtain certain medical information. (There have

been cases in which doctors haven't been able to properly treat a patient because they, and the patient, lacked medical information on the biological parents. In these cases, heredity was more important than environment.) Sometimes the reason is stated as a psychological one—the adoptee's great desire to find that old necessity, *identity.*

Practically everyone who is concerned with searching agrees on two things: One, it should not be undertaken by anyone who has not yet become an adult. Which means that you, if you're a young person, have plenty of time to think before you decide what you're going to do. And two, if an adoptee *is* successful in finding the name and address of a birth parent, it is wise to ask an intermediary—a close friend, a doctor, a religious professional, or someone familiar with the study of human behavior—to approach the parent first, to break the news gently and to ask the parent if she or he wants to meet the person who always seems to end up being referred to as the "long lost" son or daughter.

There are several organizations around the country that exist to help adoptees and, particularly, adoptees who are searching. One of the best-known is ALMA, which stands for Adoptees' Liberty Movement Association and which has its headquarters in New York City. ALMA gives guidance and assistance to its members, most of whom are adoptees over the age of eighteen, about mutual problems and especially about searching. The organization has what it calls a Reunion Registry, in which adoptees who are searching and biological parents who are searching can send in basic information (such as date and place of birth, name of hospital, and other details) in hopes that both can be matched up.

A good source of information on many aspects of adoption—not just searching, but other forms of support as well, along with reading lists and the names and addresses of national organizations—is a booklet called "Adoption in America: Help Directory." The booklet was especially created for the public television program called "Adoption in America."

Searches have varying outcomes. Some, of course, have no outcomes at all, for the searcher is unsuccessful in finding the birth parent. Some are disappointing because the parent is uncomfortable and sees the "reunion" as some kind of a threat to the "new life" she or he has created since the birth of the baby. Some biological parents, when found, turn out to be mentally or physically ill, and some turn out to be not very nice people at all. Many of the adoptees who have searched successfully, though, describe their searches as very satisfying. For they now know the things they set out to learn: what their biological parents were like, and why they were placed for adoption. And they are likely to discover that those parents were just ordinary people, and that there would be no further need in fantasizing about them. Some find, as well, that they have brothers and sisters, or half-brothers and half-sisters, whom they never knew about.

A search involves more than the adoptee and the biological parents. The adoptive parents are involved too. Some of them may encourage their children to find out, when they become adults, more about their origins.

Some, however, may think of searching as a threat to themselves. "If we've been good parents," they may wonder, "why does our child need to search?" The organization in Philadelphia that held meetings for adoptive parents has found that, in the beginning, "The most intense concern" raised by the parents "was the possibility that the children might seek out their birth parents." The fear, said the report, was that if an adoptee found her or his biological parents, the adoptive parents might somehow find themselves bumped out of their place in the adoptee's feelings.

But then an interesting thing happened. As the parents talked about this and other worries they shared (but that they had never discussed before), their fears seemed to disappear. They started seeing the situation through their children's eyes. And while they continued to be apprehensive about the child's future, said the report, their "concerns about loss of their children's love seemed abated. . . . There was general agreement that an adopted adult should have a right to know his original name."

Experts in adoption tend to agree that searching does little, if any, harm to the adoptive family. The

group of Californians who studied adoption concluded in their book on the subject that if there is
one flat statement that can be made, "it is that a
primary benefit of the reunion experience is the
strengthening of the adoptive family relationships."

An organization in North Carolina named Adoptees Together, which helps adults who want to
search, puts it another way: "We are not seeking to
replace the family relationship we have with the
parents who raised us, nor are we seeking another
set of parents. We are seeking only for the truth of
our past. Adoptive parents may not want to face
the fact that their child may have questions about
their origins, but the fact is there. The adoption of
a child does not imply lifetime control of our
thoughts and desires, just as giving birth to a child
does not guarantee his love or loyalty. We do put
a high priority on the needs and feelings of our
adoptive parents. We offer assurance that knowing
our birth parents will not decrease our love but will
add to it. When we are adopted, we do not auto-
matically shut off all concerns of our past. The past
is a basic, normal concern that is not indigenous to
adopted persons."

There is another result that comes from the
search, and it is one that many adoptees say is the
most rewarding one. That is the special, personal
satisfaction that comes from making the search in
the first place. A search for anything is like a
journey—in fact, many adoptees who have searched

use that term in describing what they have done. And often people who make exciting journeys realize that what they learn along the way, about themselves and the world around them, is often more important than what they learn at the end.

Fifteen

No Longer Alone

As an adoptee, you're going to get (and maybe already have received) a lot of free advice from other people on the subject of how you should feel about being adopted. Maybe you've noticed that some of that advice, perhaps even too much of it, has come from this book. We all like to think that we're qualified to tell other people how they should conduct their lives.

A lot of information on adoption and being adopted is provided by your parents. A big part of the job of being a parent, after all, consists of dispensing advice. Some of the information comes from inside your own head, as you have experiences and emotions and file them away mentally and later retrieve them and sort them out and use them in your day-to-day life. And an increasing amount of information and advice comes from those who call themselves the "militant adoptees." These people are more than likely to be found working in organizations that are very much in favor of searching and changing the laws that presently require that birth records be sealed. The militants are likely, too, to be the people you'll read and hear about in newspapers and magazines and on television, because the positions they take are considered newsworthy and controversial.

The militants come in differing degrees of militancy. Some, like Adoptees Together, recognize that not all adoptees are interested in searching. That group says, in a brochure describing itself: "Some adoptees argue they feel no need to seek out information about their biological background. That is their right. But, hopefully, this will not be a basis for denying equal rights to those of us who do."

Others among the militants seem to feel that there's something wrong with any adult adoptee who has *not* searched. Some of them seem to hold the very practice of adoption in contempt. "Adoption is slavery," says Florence Fisher, who founded ALMA. She also refers to adoptees as "pawns" in a chess game played by social agencies and parents.

Some of the other militants refer to themselves as "orphans," even though they are grown up. One of the best-known of the writers on the subject, Betty Jean Lifton, tends to make all-encompassing statements about adoptees, and ignores the fact that adopted persons can be just as different among themselves as members of any other category of humanity. ("Many" adoptees are homosexual, she writes, and "the desire to search has always been there" in an adoptee's mind. There is no scientific evidence to support either of these statements.)

There is militancy on the other side, too. Writer and social worker Eda LeShan, who is an adoptive mother, wrote a magazine article in *Woman's Day* not long ago that roundly condemned searching. "I am deeply concerned about those who search for their biological roots," wrote Ms. LeShan. "I'm not bothered by the fact that they *want* to—that seems entirely natural—but by the fact that they *give* in to this impulse. If psychology has taught us anything, it has made clear that we are almost constantly bombarded by impulses to which we must learn *not* to give in! There are times when we'd like to hit someone, times when we'd love to steal, times when we feel like saying something cruel. Maturity comes when we learn to control such impulses."

Adoption, and particularly searching, are very emotional topics. Many of the people who are concerned with these subjects—because they are adoptees, or adoptive parents, or biological parents, or social workers—are so emotionally involved that they assume *everyone* thinks the same way they do— or, even worse, that everyone *should* think the same way they do or else there's something wrong with them. But adoptees are not all stamped from the same mold like fast-food hamburgers. Not all adoptees think of themselves as "pawns" or "orphans," and not all of them think of the system that gave them loving homes and families as "slavery." Nor, by any stretch of the imagination, should the honest, understandable desire by some adoptees to find out more about their origins be thought of as a bad impulse, one that's on the same level with an urge to steal.

In the midst of all the emotion, it is important to remember, again, that being adopted affects different people in different ways. Some people do remember that. Vicki Campbell, an adoptee, was testifying not long ago before a state legislature committee that was considering changing the adoption law. She said:

"Although I felt secure in the love of my adoptive parents, another part of me always felt rejected and abandoned. I was also plagued with much guilt, as I felt wrong in having these feelings and questions. I never shared any of this with my parents, for several reasons: fear of hurting them, fear of more rejection, and the anxieties of my guilt. My search was frustrating, to say the least, and at times seemed futile. During this time, I felt emotionally drained and very alone in my search. Having others in my situation to converse with helped tremendously. The support and understanding of other adoptees and birth parents was of great importance during this time. . . .

"While I realize that all adoptees do not desire information about their origin, those of us who do should be able to obtain it without going through a frustrating search. We are being denied our most precious right—the truth of our beginning. This can only be defined as horrendously unjust. We are not adopted children; we are responsible adults and can handle whatever we may encounter in our search. . . ."

There is a good chance that in the future—perhaps by the time the readers of this book have reached voting age—some of the frustrations that Vicki Campbell spoke about will be lessened. The laws and customs that impose such a thick veil of secrecy on the adoptee's earliest moments of life are slowly being changed; it is very likely that adopted persons who feel a need to find out more, and who are mature enough to act responsibly, will be able to find it. Another very important change is already in the process of taking place: Adoptees, who in the past might easily have felt that their frustrations, fears, and questions belonged somehow to them, uniquely, now know—largely because of all the noise that the militants have been making—that they are not alone. We now know that, even though it's wrong to say "all" adoptees feel this way or that, it is not unusual to wonder about rejection, or origins. As Vicki Campbell said, knowing that others are having the same experiences helps a lot.

As the veil is lifted, each side of the adoptive triangle will find some of its basic ideas challenged. It should become obvious to everyone involved that the only policy that stands a chance of working from now on, for anyone in the triangle, is the policy of complete honesty. The fairy-tale stories of the past—about birth parents who were married and who died painlessly in accidents (but only after

being told that their child was being placed in the
world's happiest adoptive home)—won't work any
longer. Another technique that won't work is silence—the sort of silence that sometimes exists
between the adoptee and her parents, with each of
them having questions to ask or feelings to express,
and each knowing the other has something to say,
but each not asking or saying anything, for fear of
"hurting feelings" or of appearing to be ungrateful.
Those examples of not-quite-honesty never did
work, really, but the members of the adoptive triangle always used to *pretend* that they did.

Adoptive parents will have to realize that the
child's curiosity about his origins is a wonderful,
normal thing and not a sign that the adoption isn't
working or that they've been failures as parents.
Biological parents will have to realize that there is
no longer any guarantee that the children they
place for adoption won't someday appear to ask
questions that are very important to them. And
adoptees will have to realize that they now have a
powerful opportunity, one that did not exist before,
to go back in time and find out about their ethnic
heritage, about their forebears, about why they
have brown eyes or big feet, and about some of the
countless bits of information, most of them trivial
but all of them interesting, that go into shaping a
human being's history. Adoptees also will have the
opportunity, if they want to take it, to reconstruct
the events and people who brought them into the
world, and to seek the answer to the question about

why they were adopted in the first place.

And adoptees have a powerful opportunity to conduct their search in any other way they like, or even to not conduct a search at all, if that is what they want. Like adoptees and like people in general, not all searches are similar. Searching does not always mean tracking down your biological parents in order to find your "identity." Searching can also mean looking within your own mind and counting the feelings, ambitions, angers, sensitivities, frustrations, desires, hurts, experiences, evil thoughts, loves, lonelinesses, humors, worthy thoughts, proudnesses, shames, skills, satisfactions, and most of all the hopes that go into making you the unique person you are. And then recognizing all those qualities for what they are and thinking about what you're going to do with them for the rest of your life.

Some people, by the time they become teenagers, are saddled with the attribute of being very good-looking. Part of their growing-up process includes figuring out how to incorporate that attribute of being very good-looking into their lives. It's the same with being very tall, or very short, or very average in appearance, or very musically inclined, or an apparent whiz at mathematics, or an apparent nonwhiz at anything in the classroom; or with being the only girl in a large family of bratty boys, or with being adopted. Like all the other qualities, being adopted is part of living, of your life. It is not a handicap unless you're the victim of some very special circumstances (like really cruel parents, which isn't very likely) or unless you, yourself, *work* at making it a handicap.

You can see that I'm a much stronger believer in the sort of searching that goes on within your own mind than I am in the sort that results in seeking out your birth parents. That's just the way I am (or, at least, the way I am *now*. It's entirely possible that some day I'll change).

I've done some checking into the past. While it wouldn't fit a militant adoptee's definition of "searching" (one of them told me so, in no uncertain terms), it has been enough for me. Several years ago I found myself in the town where I had stayed for a couple of months, at a public adoption agency, between the time I was born and the time I was adopted. Almost on the spur of the moment (although I had been thinking about it, consciously and subconsciously, for years) I picked up a telephone and called the agency. "Come on over," said the voice at the other end, "and let's talk."

The woman with whom I talked was pleasant and nice and understanding about my nervousness. She had a sheet of paper in front of her, and she read the details to me: The first and middle names I had when I was born, but not the last name; the place and time of birth; my weight (I certainly have grown, I thought); a few facts about my biological mother and her family, but nothing that could be used to identify them (she was five-feet-five inches tall, said the woman, had light brown hair, and was "pretty"). There were even fewer facts about my biological father (he was an engineer with the state highway department; they said he had died not long after I was born. He was said to have been "slender," which was a solid argument against heredity in the "nature versus nurture" controversy, since I'm definitely not slender). A doctor who knew my mother's family had said, back then, that the family was "honest and honorable."

The pleasant woman lifted her eyes from the sheet of paper. "Your parents were not married," she said.

I thought: So much for the story about the college professors who were happily married and wanted to travel. But I had figured out, on my own, the falseness of that story a long time ago. The woman's announcement was certainly not a surprise to me.

Some adoptees would have taken the few facts I received that day and used them as the starting point for a detailed search—one that, they hoped, would not end until the name of that brown-haired, pretty woman could be found, and perhaps the woman herself as well. For some reason, I did not do that. The information I got that day seemed to be enough.

It was several years later that I discovered, quite by accident, what seems to be a difference of opinion about my birthday. I'd been celebrating it all along on February 23. A few years after my adoptive mother died, however, I ran across her diary for the year in which I was born. I went through it, day by day, waiting to see what she would say about me. Of course, there was nothing on February 23, since she and my father didn't know I even existed until several months later, when they adopted me.

On June 23, there was the first mention: "Jack [her nickname for my father] and I went to Greensboro [where the agency was] to visit the home. Saw a baby we liked quite a bit." Three days later, she returned to Greensboro to take another look. On June 27, she wrote: "Still undecided about the baby. Quite a worry." Apparently if I was going to be a Chosen Baby, I wouldn't be Chosen right off the bat. (Or was it some *other* baby she was undecided about?)

June 30: "Brought baby home! Jack and I drove over and made up our minds the minute we saw him." Finally, they picked me out! Maybe I wasn't the June 23 and 27 baby. On the next day, they named me.

Apparently I kept my parents pretty busy after that, because there weren't many entries in the diary. (I got a "dark blue English carriage—not new" on July 13.) But there was another diary, for the following year, and it was one in which my mother had made entries for me, as if I were writing them down. "Slept until 7:30," said the diary for January 9. "This pleases Mother." Apparently I had developed the habit of waking up very early and making sure everybody else got up, too. As I read through this diary, I came across the notation that "I was eleven months old today." The date was February 2—impossible if my birthday was really February 23. I looked again through other documents. In a scrapbook, my mother had written: "Baby's first tooth appeared the day he was six months old, Sept. 2." In the front of the scrapbook there was a place for the date of my birth. When I looked closely at it, I could see that the original entry had been erased and "February 23" put in its place.

So apparently I was born on March 2 rather than February 23. The reason for the confusion, I think, is a simple one: Changing the date was something that was done often back then. It was another way of ensuring that the adoptee would not be able to probe into his past—another fold of the veil that was supposed to separate forever the adopted person's two lives.

For me, the difference in birth dates is a pleasant mystery, and one that I have no great ambition to "solve." I am quite comfortable with two birthdays. Not being sure which is the real one has not caused me any identity problems. In fact, since I made the discovery I have requested that my family give me *two* birthday dinners, one each February 23 (when the specialty is cherry pie, my favorite) and one each March 2 (when I get lasagna, which is also my favorite), and which helps explain why I'm not "slender" like my biological father.

The important point to remember, I think, is that when you're ready, you can do any sort of searching you want to do. You can search the four corners of the world for the people who are important to your life, and you can search deep within yourself for the qualities that are just as meaningful. You don't have to do what other people think is fashionable. Now, as never before, an adopted person has the ability and tools to figure out what his or her identity really is.

The search, like any big, important trip to a place you've never seen before, is an exciting prospect. You never know what you'll find, and you don't have any idea of what you'll be like when the search is over. Important searches and journeys almost always result in changes in the people who're conducting them. Just like the early peoples who explored the United States, first the Indians and then the settlers who moved westward the width of the country, you learn a lot along the way. *That* learning, perhaps as much as anything else, is what goes into making and finding an identity—whether you're adopted, or whether you're one of those people who's not quite so special.

For Further Reading

Some publications and organizations that might be helpful in understanding more about adoption:

Books

Berman, Claire. *We Take This Child: A Candid Look at Modern Adoption.* Garden City, NY: Doubleday, 1974.

Carney, Ann. *No More Here and There: Adopting the Older Child.* Chapel Hill, NC: University of North Carolina Press, 1976.

Fisher, Florence. *The Search for Anna Fisher.* New York: Arthur Fields, 1973.

Lifton, Betty Jean. *Twice Born: Memoirs of an Adopted Daughter.* New York: McGraw Hill, 1975.

McNamara, Joan. *The Adoption Adviser.* New York: Hawthorn, 1975.

Sorosky, Arthur D., Annette Baran, and Reuben Pannor. *The Adoption Triangle.* Garden City, NY: Anchor Press/ Doubleday, 1979.

Other Publications

Adoption in America: Help Directory. The North American Council on Adoptable Children, 1346 Connecticut Avenue, N.W., Washington, D.C. 1980. (The directory contains much information on agencies that deal with adoption, names and addresses of groups that promote searching, and a reading list.)

Bernard, Viola W. "Adoption." Chapter 25 in the *American Handbook of Psychiatry,* vol. 1. New York: Basic Books, 1974.

Marquis, Kathlyn S. and Richard A. Detweiler. "The Adoptive Experience: Its Effects on Attributions to Self and Others." Unpublished ms. Department of Psychology, Drew University, Madison, NJ, 1981.

Phillips, Maxine. *Adopting a Child.* Public Affairs Pamphlet No. 585. Public Affairs Committee, 381 Park Avenue South, New York, NY, 1980.

Rights of Adopted Children. A Report to the 1981 General Assembly of North Carolina. State of North Carolina Legislative Research Commission, State Legislative Building, Raleigh, NC, 1980.

Organizations

Adoptees' Liberty Movement Association. Florence Fisher, president. P.O. Box 154, Washington Bridge Station, New York, NY, 10033. (A membership organization of adoptees and biological parents that encourages and gives advice on searching. ALMA maintains a "reunion registry databank" for persons "separated through adoption who wish to be reunited.")

Child Welfare League of America, Inc. 67 Irving Place, New York, NY, 10003.

Concerned United Birthparents, Inc. P.O. Box 573, Milford, MA 01757; or P.O. Box 7482, Philadelphia, PA 19101; or P.O. Box 115, Haddon Heights, NJ, 08035. (". . . a support/activist organization for men and women who have surrendered children to adoption. We also have an auxiliary membership for nonbirthparents who support our goal to humanize adoption.")

North Carolina Adoptees Together, Inc. Holly H. Hill, founder. Route 1, Box 30 B 5, Climax, NC, 27233.

("... a statewide search group that assists members of the adoption 'triangle' in searching." One of several such groups that exist on the state level.)

Orphan Voyage. Joan Paton, coordinator. RD 1, Box 153 A, Cedaredge, CO, 81413. (Purposes are, among other things, to "set up lines of communication in the adoption population between those needing help and those able to give it; to encourage open attitudes in the nonadoption population; to look for solutions from the coordination and cooperation of the three elements of the adoption population . . .")

Index